Nietzsche for Breakfast

Jon Ferguson

Huge Jam Publishing
2024

Copyright © 2024 Jon Ferguson
All rights reserved.
ISBN: 978-1-916604-21-6

PREFACE (1994)

Friedrich Nietzsche and I have one thing in common: we both came from homes in which Christianity was the center of the family. His father was a pastor; mine started the first "branch" of the Mormon Church in Orinda, California with services held in our livingroom.

From my religious upbringing, only two things stuck. First, that Jesus was probably a nice guy, and second, that man should seek the truth. The "truth" part meant for me that one should not be satisfied with believing what his culture had fed him. I suspect Nietzsche left his youth with a similar outlook.

The fact that from age ten to sixteen I was a sports fanatic might have led me to where I am today. During Sunday School I used to sneak out to the family car and listen to San Francisco 49er football games and Giants baseball games on the radio. Hence I missed out on a lot of the detailed teachings, the hard symbols, the "devil" part of the deal, and the nails of guilt that pinned most of my church acquaintances to the Christian wall for life. For me the prophets weren't Moses, Moroni, Mormon, and Methuselah; they were John Brodie,

Gene Washington, Willie Mays, and Juan Marichal. They played with balls, bats, and shoulder pads, not with good, evil, and original sin.

I did stay in the Mormon group through high school and for two years at Brigham Young University, the Mormon controlled institution in Provo, Utah. Then at age twenty, I was "called" by the Church to be a missionary in Argentina. This calling is the case for all Mormon men of good and less-than-good standing. Here my smooth ride on the theological treadmill ended. As a missionary I was supposed to tell the world that "I know the Church is true", "that Jesus is the Christ" (this formula struck me early as smelling tautological), and that "Joseph Smith restored the true church of God to the earth". This I could not say for the simple reason that Mormonism was the only thing I'd ever known and truth looked maybe to be many different things for many people.

I agreed to spend three months in what was then called "The Language Training Mission" with the 100 or so other missionaries who were headed to Spanish-speaking countries. In the LTM we spent sixteen hours a day studying the scriptures and learning Spanish. We prayed over thirty times a day (when we got up, before breakfast, after breakfast, before the morning class etc).

Our teachers were all ex-missionaries with little philosophical training and the questions I started asking about "knowledge", "truth", "meaning", and "ethics" got to be too much for them. Finally, towards the end of my three months, they sent me to Salt Lake City to meet with Spencer W. Kimball, who at that time was the second highest authority in the Mormon kingdom (he later became the "President" or "living Prophet"). We spent an hour together. He did all the talking and did absolutely nothing to help me weed through my questions. A few days later I was the only missionary not to get on the plane to South America. I went back to BYU and took all the philosophy classes I could. I wanted the truth.

Like Nietzsche, the more I studied the less I thought truth was something to be had by man. I began to think that all philosophical systems were no more provable than the Mormon religion I had ceased to believe in and give my money to.

After three years of study the only philosopher I still enjoyed reading was Nietzsche. I thought him the least deluded and the most amusing. I left America in 1973 at age twenty-three and have lived in Switzerland ever since. This break with the homeland was also a split with the formal academic world.

Here I've made a living playing and coaching basketball, writing a column in the Lausanne paper, teaching English in a Swiss high school, and periodically painting pictures. For twenty years Nietzsche's books have been in a pocket or hand when I stroll along the shores of Lac Leman with my dog. I want to show you why I still read him and show you in a most edible way. Hence "Nietzsche for Breakfast". He might help your digestion. He has aided mine and has nourished me through many a day.

JF
St. Luc, Switzerland
October, 1994

1

WHAT MAKES NIETZSCHE DIFFERENT FROM OTHER 'PHILOSOPHICAL TYPES'?

To use an American football metaphor, tackling Friedrich Nietzsche is not like tackling a two-hundred-and-sixty-pound fullback; it's more like trying to bring down a fleet flankerback who's running loose in the open field on an end-around. Most philosophers build systems. The reader must first learn what the words mean, then he follows the thinker straight ahead to a series of "logical conclusions". This is how one approaches a Kant or a Descartes or a Spinoza. With Nietzsche, one starts and ends on slippery ground. He fakes, he jumps, he backs up, he takes off his uniform, showers, then starts again somewhere in the middle of the game. There are no beginnings to learn and ends to swallow; there is a man in the face of the world... an ever-changing man in the midst of an ever-changing world. He does not give answers because there are no answers to be given. This accounts for his popularity in some circles and his unpopularity in others. Historically people have wanted to know "how things are". With Nietzsche there are no things.

With most philosophers you know how much time is left in the game, what the score is, the players' names and numbers, and who the winners and losers are. With Nietzsche there is no scoreboard, the names and numbers are in constant flux, and choosing a winner is like crowning a pig in a Miss Universe contest. We're all in the same glorious sty. Let's listen to Nietzsche tell us why:

Source of knowledge. — Throughout tremendous periods of time the intellect begot nothing but errors; some of them proved useful and preservative of the species: he who came upon them or inherited them fought his fight for himself and his posterity with greater good fortune. These articles of belief, which have been repeatedly handed down and have finally become almost a basic component of the human species, are for example the following: that there are enduring things, that there are identical things, that there are things, material, bodies, that a thing is what it appears to be, that our willing is free, that what is good for me is good in itself. Deniers and doubters of these propositions appeared only of late — truth, as the feeblest form of knowledge, appeared only very late. It seemed one was incapable of living with truth, our organism was adapted to the opposite; all its higher functions, the perceptions of the senses and every kind of sensation in general worked in concert with those primevally incorporated fundamental errors. More: those propositions became even within the domain of knowledge the norms according to which one meted out 'true' and 'untrue' — right into the remotest regions of pure logic. Thus the strength of items of knowledge lies, not in their degree of truth, but in their age, their incorporatedness, their character as a condition of life. Where life and knowledge seem to come into contradiction there is never any serious contest; doubt and denial here counts as madness... (GS 110)

To repeat what Nietzsche considers the "errors" of thinking that have taken over most philosophical discourse: *that there are enduring things, that there are things, that there are identical things, material, bodies, that a thing is what it appears to be, that our willing is free, that what is good for me is good in itself.* In considering these things "untrue" — "errors" — Nietzsche may not be alone, but he sets himself apart from most others.

His view of thinking itself puts him in a different ballpark:

Having kept a close eye on philosophers and read between their lines for a sufficient length of time, I tell myself: the greater part of their conscious thinking must still be counted among the instinctive activities, and this is so even in the case of philosophical thinking... Just as the act of being born plays no part in the procedure and progress of heredity, so 'being conscious' is in no decisive sense the opposite of the instinctive — most of a philosopher's conscious thinking is secretly directed and compelled into definite channels by his instincts. (BGE 3)

Not only is thinking mostly some kind of instinctive activity, with Nietzsche there is no "I" that "thinks". There is no firm ego or subject that "thinks" just like there is no "wind" that "blows"; there is "blowing", but there is no subject "wind" that creates the blowing.

Through thought the ego is posited; but hitherto one believed as ordinary people do, that in "I think" there was something of immediate certainty, and that this "I" was the given cause of thought, from which by analogy we understood all other causal relationships. However habitual and indispensable this fiction may have become now — that in itself proves nothing against its imaginary origin: a belief can be a condition of life and nonetheless false. (WP 483)

A philosopher who does not believe that "he" "thinks" is a "thinker" apart. Most philosophers pride themselves in the depths and clarity of "their" thinking. They think they have taken thinking farther than their predecessors or at least in some way made clearer the ideas of those before them. For Nietzsche, thinking is nothing to be proud of; it happens like the wind happens. There is no doer that does with Nietzsche.

It is belief in the living and thinking as the only effective force — in will, in intention — it is belief that every event is a deed, that every deed presupposes a doer, it is belief in the "subject". Is this belief in the concept of subject and attribute not a great stupidity? (WP 550)

Nietzsche different from other thinkers? Listen to the air move as he swings this baseball bat at traditional "thinking":

There are still harmless self-observers who believe 'immediate certainties' exist, for example, 'I think'... But I shall reiterate a hundred times that 'immediate certainty', like 'absolute knowledge' and 'thing in itself', contains a contradiction in adjecto (contradiction in terms)... when I analyze the event expressed in the sentence 'I think' I acquire a series of rash assertions which are difficult, perhaps impossible, to prove — for example, that it is I which thinks, that thinking is an activity and operation on the part of an entity thought of as a cause, that an I exists, finally that what is designated by 'thinking' has already been determined — that I know what thinking is... In this way the philosopher acquires in place of that 'immediate certainty'... a series of metaphysical questions... 'Whence do I take the concept thinking? Why do I believe in cause and effect? What gives me the right to speak of an I... an I as cause... an I as cause of thoughts? (BGE 16)

And this thump:

As for the superstitions of the logicians, I shall never tire of underlining a concise little fact which these superstitious people are loath to admit – namely, that a thought comes when 'it' wants, not when 'I' want;

so that it is a falsification of the facts to say: the subject 'I' is the condition of the predicate 'think'. It thinks: but that this 'it' is precisely that famous old 'I' is, to put it mildly, only an assumption, an assertion, above all not an 'immediate certainty'. (BGE 17)

To understand simply what is being said here, just try, yourself, not to think for thirty seconds. No luck right? You can't turn off thinking. The "I" — if it's there at all — surely doesn't control the "thinking". What was or is a "certainty" for so many thinkers, is, for Nietzsche, a great uncertainty, and more, a source of numerous errors which we will stumble on later.

2

HOW DOES NIETZSCHE VIEW TRADITIONAL PHILOSOPY AND OTHER PHILOSOPHERS?

All philosophers have the common failing of starting out from man as he is now and thinking they can reach their goal through an analysis of him. They involuntarily think of 'man' as an 'aeterna veritas', as something that remains constant in the midst of all flux, as a sure measure of things. Everything the philosopher has declared about man is, however, at bottom no more than a testimony as to the man of a very limited period of time. Lack of historical sense is the family failing of all philosophers... (HA 2)

Nietzsche says that thinkers who think they are in a position to reveal truth about human being are destined to fail and have always failed. Any philosopher's perspective is so impossibly small in the great picture of human development:

They (philosophers) will not learn that man has become, that the faculty of cognition has become; while some of them would have it that the whole world is spun out of this faculty of cognition. Now, everything essential in the development of mankind took place in primeval times, long before the 4,000 years we more or less know about; during these years mankind may well not have altered very much. But the philosopher here sees 'instincts' in man as he now is and assumes that these belong to the unalterable facts of mankind, and to that extent could provide a key to the understanding of the world in general: the whole of teleology is constructed by speaking of the man of the last four millennia as of an eternal man towards whom all things in the world have had a natural relationship from the time he began. But everything has become: there are no eternal facts, just as there are no absolute truths. (HA 2)

Just as the philosopher's perspective is an obstacle not to be overcome, his eye is fixed on a goal — to understand the world — in a way that is wrong; i.e.

To solve everything at a stroke, with a single word — that was the secret desire... 'There is a riddle to be solved': thus did the goal of life appear to the eye of the philosopher; the first thing to do was to find the riddle and to compress the problem of the world into the simplest riddle-form. The boundless ambition and exultation of being the 'unriddler of the world' constituted the thinker's dreams: nothing seemed worthwhile if it was to the means of bringing everything to a conclusion for him! (D 547)

Nietzsche is pointed in a direction that few philosophers have dared to go. Instead of seeing man as the focus, the centre, the brain of the universe, he is imagining the most real possibility that man is but a dot — an unknowing dot — in the vast *(O so vast!)* cosmos. Not only does he intellectualise this possibility, but he feels it, he breathes it, his heart beats it. Maybe, even likely, the history of Western thinking has been a great exercise in delusion, in sealing humanity in a warm airtight balloon that protects us from the raw, brute, simple fact of our being. To imagine what he is saying about traditional philosophy (and religion) is perhaps the most difficult thing to grasp with Nietzsche. But we must grasp it first — now — in order to see what his vision is all about.

Nietzsche sees a "freer" nature over the horizon, i.e. a kind of man who does not hide himself in the aforesaid cloak. Listen to him talk of such a man:

The great liberation comes for those who are thus fettered suddenly, like the shock of an earthquake: the youthful soul is all at once convulsed, torn loose, torn away — it itself does not know what is happening. A drive and impulse rules and masters it like a command; a will and desire awakens to go off, anywhere, at any cost; a vehement dangerous curiosity for an undiscovered world flames and flickers in all its senses. 'Better to die than to go on living here' — thus resounds the imperious voice and temptation: and this 'here', this 'at home' is everything it has hitherto loved, a lightning bolt of contempt for what it called 'duty', a rebellious, arbitrary, volcanically erupting desire for travel, strange places, estrangement, coldness, soberness, frost, a hatred for love, perhaps a desecrating blow and glance backwards to where it formerly loved and worshipped, perhaps a hot blush of shame at what it has just done and at the same time an exultation that it has done it, a drunken, inwardly exultant shudder that betrays that a victory has been won — a victory? Over what? Over whom? An enigmatic question-packed, questionable victory, but the first nonetheless: such bad and painful things are part of the history of the great liberation... With a wicked laugh he turns round whatever he finds veiled and through some sense of shame or other spared and pampered: he puts to the test what these things look like when they are reversed... Behind all this toiling and weaving — for he is restlessly and aimlessly on his way as if in a desert — stands the question-mark of a more and more perilous curiosity. 'Can all values not be turned round? And is good perhaps evil? And God only an invention and finesse of the Devil? Is everything perhaps in the last resort false? And if we are deceived, are we not for that very reason also deceivers? Must we not be deceivers?' — Such thoughts as these tempt him and lead him on, ever further away, ever further down. Solitude encircles and embraces him, ever more threatening, suffocating, heart-tightening, that terrible goddess and mater saeva cupidinum — but who today knows what solitude is? (HA Preface 3-6)

Here the reader might rightly (for himself) ask: why go on? Who wants the solitude Friedrich Nietzsche is getting at? My answer — my only answer — is that as I said in the preface, if we really want 'truth', we must plough on, even to 'untruth' or... or... who knows?... even joy.

3

ON NIETZSCHE'S VIEW OF METAPHYSICS

Metaphysics is the study of or the getting at the "real". Obviously most people don't bother with such thoughts about what is and isn't "real," because "a cat is a cat" and a "tree is a tree". Philosophers, on the other hand, have tried in various ways to cut behind the world to apprehend a "higher", "deeper", "truer" reality. Religions do the same. (Physics too is in a sense metaphysics: the goal is to reveal raw reality. The world surely looks very different under a high-powered microscope or through an astronomer's telescope). Nietzsche, in *Human, All Too Human*, succinctly explains what he sees to be the origin of metaphysics:

Misunderstanding of the dream. — Man of the ages of barbarous primordial culture believed that in the dream he was getting to know a second real world: here is the origin of all metaphysics. Without the dream, one would have had no occasion to divide the world into two. The dissection into body and soul is also connected with the oldest idea of the dream, likewise the postulation of a life of the soul, thus the origin of all belief in spirits and probably also of the belief in gods. "The dead live on, for they appear to the living in dreams": that was the conclusion one formerly drew, throughout many millennia. (HA 5)

Nietzsche would never deny the possibility that a "higher", "deeper", or "truer" world might in fact exist; he just says that the actual business of really knowing such a thing is beyond man's capacity.

Metaphysical world. — It is true, there could be a metaphysical world; the absolute possibility of it is hardly to be disputed. We behold all things through the human head and cannot cut off this head; while the question nonetheless remains what of the world would still be there if one had cut it off. This is a purely scientific problem and one not very well calculated to bother people overmuch; but all that has hitherto made metaphysical assumption valuable, terrible, delightful to them, all that has begotten these assumptions, is passion, error and self-deception; the worst of all methods of acquiring knowledge, not the best of all, have taught belief in them. When one has disclosed these methods as the foundation of all extant religions and metaphysical systems one has refuted them! Then the possibility still remains over; but one can do absolutely nothing with it, not to speak of letting happiness, salvation and life depend on the gossamer of such a possibility. — For one could assert nothing at all of the metaphysical world except that it was a being-other; it would be a thing with negative qualities. — Even if the existence of such a world were never so well demonstrated, it is certain that knowledge of it would be the most useless of all knowledge: more useless even than knowledge of the chemical composition of water must be to the sailor in danger of shipwreck. (HA 9)

This passage exemplifies Nietzsche's will to look life in face and accept only what can honestly be accepted: first, the human head has only itself to go on and there's no guarantee that what goes on inside it corresponds with truth; second, if there was another realm of being, it would be just that — "another" — and hence unknowable for us of this world; and third, even if it did become knowable it would do nothing to get us through this life.

The book *The Will of Power* is a compilation of excerpts from Nietzsche's notebooks from 1883 to 1888. In it we find some of his most succinct and biting howls against the business of metaphysics:

If one is a philosopher as men have always been philosophers, one cannot see what has been or what becomes — one sees only what is. But since nothing is, all that was left to the philosopher as his 'world' was the imaginary. (WP 570)

Psychology of metaphysics. — This world is apparent: consequently there is a true world; — this world is conditional: consequently there is an unconditioned world; — this world is full of contradiction: consequently there is a world free of contradiction; —this world is a world of becoming: consequently there is a world of being: — all false conclusions (blind trust in reason: if A exists, then the opposite concept B must also exist). It is suffering that inspires these conclusions: fundamentally they are desires that such a world should exist; in the same way, to imagine another, more valuable world is an expression of hatred for a world that makes one suffer: the ressentiment of metaphysicians against actuality is here creative... (WP 579)

Being — we have no idea of it apart from the idea 'living'. — How can anything dead 'be'? (WP 582)

...There would be nothing that could be called knowledge if thought did not first re-form the world in this way into 'things', into what is self-identical.

Only because there is thought is there untruth. (WP 574)

The 'real world', however one has hitherto conceived it — it has always been the apparent world once again. (WP 566)

All efforts toward metaphysics are limited by the human head and this head always sees "things", things that "are". But what is isn't because everything is always becoming, changing, part of a great flux.

I once was seated in a restaurant in Geneva across from a physicist at the CERN, the European Center for Nuclear Research. I asked him about the very thing Nietzsche is talking about. "Does modern physics believe there is really such a 'thing' as an atom or an electron or a particle?" He calmly responded that they no longer believe in 'things' but in 'forces', i.e. they can't find any real objects, parts, or particles as such, but only fields of forces and motion. Naturally this brought out a twinkle to my Nietzsche-reading eyes.

Imagine for a moment that everything the human eye sees is really not static as we see it, but in a state of flux as Nietzsche suggests. All talk about thingness, this "thing" and that "thing" becomes ridiculous or rather becomes just an effort of the human mind to "stop the world", to try to make sense of and give order to what really can't be made sense of. This is what Nietzsche is trying to say. This is the "honesty" with which he confronts human being. Let's stop — he says — making statements that are finally mythic. If we're going to really think, let's think all the way and stop deluding ourselves with half-truths or non-truths. If "truth" is something out of man's reach, let's admit it, look it in the face, and "live" with it. If a cat is not a cat, i.e. if we cannot "know" the infinity of becoming, if the human mind is not equipped to fathom beyond the apparent, surface world, so be it. But let's be honest and put metaphysics in the garbage with the broken vacuum and the empty tin can.

4

LANGUAGE: WHAT IS IT? HOW DOES IT RELATE TO METAPHYSICS?

Language as putative science. — The significance of language for the evolution of culture lies in this, that mankind set up in language a separate world beside the other world, a place it took to be so firmly set that, standing upon it, it could lift the rest of the world off its hinges and make itself master of it. To the extent that man has for long ages believed in the concepts and names of things as in aeternae veritates *he has appropriated to himself that pride by which he raised himself above the animal: he really thought that in language he possessed knowledge of the world. The sculptor of language was not so modest as to believe that he was only giving things designations, he conceived rather that with words he was expressing supreme knowledge of things; language is, in fact, the first stage of the occupation with science. Here, too, it is the belief that the truth has been found out of which the mightiest sources of energy have flowed. Very much subsequently — only now — it dawns on men that in their belief in language they have propagated a tremendous error. Happily, it is too late for the evolution of reason, which depends on this belief, to be again put back. — Logic too depends on presuppositions with which nothing in the real world corresponds, for example on the presupposition that there are identical things, that the same thing is identical at different points of time: but this science came into existence through the opposite belief (that such conditions do obtain in the real world). It is the same with mathematics, which would certainly not have come into existence if one had known from the beginning that there was in nature no exactly straight line, no real circle, no absolute magnitude. (HA 11)*

This is a mouthful — or an eyeful — or a "headful" — but it does serve to help understand Nietzsche's view of truth and metaphysics. Man has essentially forgotten that language was invented by man — not by supreme all-knowing types — and that with language man took the world apart and put it back as he saw it, breaking it down, dividing it up, and setting it up as was expedient for him. If we think back to the Geneva physicist and Nietzsche's view that there are no "things" but rather a great flux of becoming — of forces — we can see that with language man has artificially cut up what is uncuttable and called it "reality" or "truth" or "world" or "thing".

To make this idea clearer, let's imagine the world as a Jackson Pollock painting. We show it to a child, or an adult for that matter, then cut it up in a thousand pieces and ask the child to put it back together again. The "world" will still be there, i.e. the stuff of the painting, but it will hardly look like the original — it can hardly be now called "a Pollack". Language has cut up the world and put it back together again; but what it gives us is hardly "the real world".

Language — like dreams — is a culprit in the flood of erroneous thinking that has covered Western man. Nietzsche calls grammar "the metaphysics of the people". The thing, the doer, the doer that does: all falsehood born of language.

Language belongs in its origin to the age of the most rudimentary from of psychology: we find ourselves in the midst of a rude fetishism when we call to mind the basic presuppositions of the metaphysics of language — which is to say, of reason. It is this which sees everywhere deed and doer; this which believes in will as cause in general; this which believes in the 'ego' as being, in the ego as substance, and which projects its belief in the ego-substance on to all things — only thus does it create the concept 'thing'... Being is everywhere thought in, foisted on, as cause; it is only from the conception 'ego' that there follows, derivatively, the concept 'being'... At the beginning stands the great fateful error that the will is something which produces an effect — that will is a faculty... Today we know it is merely a word. (T "Reason" in Philosophy 5)

Words do not correspond to reality; they fabricate it.

We set up a word at the point at which our ignorance begins, at which we can see no further, e.g. the word 'I', the word 'do', the word 'suffer': — these are perhaps the horizon of our knowledge, but not 'truths'. (WP 482)

We think with language, hence thinking is muddled.

Ultimate solution. — We believe in reason: this, however, is the philosophy of grey concepts. Language depends on the most naïve prejudices.

Now we read disharmonies and problems into things because we think only in the form of language - and thus believe in the 'eternal truth' of 'reason' (e.g., subject, attribute, etc.)

We cease to think when we refuse to do so under

the constraint of language; we barely reach the doubt that sees this limitation as a limitation.

Rational thought is interpretation according to a scheme that we cannot throw off. (WP 522)

If we think in language and language is an obstacle to truth, more than that, if language in itself lies about the world — then language is and has always been a device which goes counter to getting at what is. In any case, for Nietzsche, what is isn't because everything is in flux. You can't catch water in a fish net.

5

WHY DOES NIETZSCHE WRITE BOOK AFTER BOOK USING THE VERY "LANGUAGE" HE SAYS IS SO UNHELPFUL?

Naturally this is a seeming paradox, but one that can be explained simply: he had a choice: either write and talk or don't write and talk. He chose the first up until 1889. Then for the last ten years of his life until his death in 1900 he neither wrote nor talked. Some say he had syphilis or some other "physical" disease and was rendered "insane". Others think he just "practiced what he had preached" and fell out of the world of speech and language. In any case, we will never know for sure because Nietzsche never told anybody why.

HOW LANGUAGE CAME ABOUT
(Nietzsche's Here for Dinner...)

Now it seems to me ... that refinement and strength of consciousness always stands in proportion to the capacity for communication of a human being (or animal), capacity for communication in turn in proportion to need for communication... Supposing this observation to be correct, I may then go on to conjecture that consciousness evolved at all under the pressure of need for communication — that it was from the very first necessary and useful only between man and man (between commanders and obeyers in particular), and also evolved only in proportion to the degree of this usefulness. Consciousness is really only a connecting network between man and man — only as such did it have to evolve: the solitary and predatory man would not have needed it. That our actions, thoughts, feelings, movements come into our consciousness — at least a part of them — is the consequence of a fearfully protracted compulsion which lay over man: as a most endangered animal he required help, protection, he required his own kind, he had to express his needs, know how to make himself understood — and for all that he first had need of 'consciousness', that is to say, himself needs to 'know' what he lacks, to 'know' how he feels, to 'know' what he is thinking. For, to say it again: man, like every living creature, thinks continually but does not know it; thinking which has become conscious is only the smallest part of it, let us say the most superficial part, the worst part — for only this conscious thinking takes place in words, that is to say in communication-signs, by which the origin of consciousness reveals itself. In short, the evolution of language and the evolution of consciousness... go hand in hand. ...The sign-inventing man is at the same time the man who is ever more sharply conscious of himself; only as a social animal did man learn to become conscious of himself — he does it still, he does it more and more. — My idea, as one can see, is that consciousness does not really belong to man as an individual, but rather to that in him which is community and herd... Our actions are fundamentally one and all in an incomparable way personal, unique, boundlessly individual, there is no doubt about that; but as soon as we translate them into consciousness they no longer seem to be... This is real phenomenalism and application of the principle of perspectives as I understand it: the nature of animal consciousness brings it about that the world of which we can become conscious is only a surface — and sign-world, a world made universal and common — that everything which becomes conscious thereby becomes shallow, thin, relatively stupid, general, sign, characteristic of the herd, that with all becoming conscious (and language) there is united a great fundamental corruption, falsification, superficializing and generalization. (GS 354)

A passage like this should be read twice because there is so much in it to digest. It's like a four-course meal in a French restaurant:

First Entrée: Language and consciousness together evolved out of man's need to communicate, his need to express what he needed to survive. "I'm hungry."

Second Entrée: As signs — words — began to fill human consciousness, these signs were no longer individual, but rather devices of the collective consciousness. "I'm hungry. Half of that rabbit is for me." Naturally what "half" or "rabbit" really is does not matter in such an exchange. Survival is what counts.

Main Course: As the collective sign-sharing consciousness grows and becomes more complex so does man's "consciousness" about himself. As Nietzsche says, *"Finally, increasing consciousness is a danger; and he who lives among the most conscious Europeans knows that it is even an illness."* We get weighed down with dictionaries and signs that we take seriously, but which are in fact nothing but thin, shallow, surface, common utensils of the herd.

Dessert: Consciousness and language are fundamental corrupters and perverters and falsifiers of what the world really is.

6

WHAT "IS" THE WORLD REALLY FOR NIETZSCHE?

It is always too soon and never too soon to ask this question. It is the question that runs through everything he says and we are saying in this book. We are trying to answer it on every page. Here is another glimpse he gives us a little later on in *The Gay Science*:

Our new 'infinity'. — How far the perspectival character of existence extends or whether an existence without interpretation, without 'meaning' would not become 'meaningless', whether on the other hand all existence is an interpreting existence — this, as is only reasonable, cannot be determined even by the most assiduous and painfully conscientious analysis and self-examination of the intellect: since in the course of this analysis the human intellect cannot avoid viewing itself in its perspectival forms and only in them. We cannot see round our own corner: it is a hopeless piece of curiosity to want to know what could exist for other species of intellect and perspective: for example, whether any kind of being could experience time in a reverse direction or alternately forwards and backwards (which would posit a different direction of life and a different conception of cause and effect). But I think that today we are at least far from the ludicrous immodesty of decreeing from out of our corner that perspectives are permissible only from out of this corner. The world has rather once again become for us 'infinite': insofar as we cannot reject the possibility that it contains in itself infinite interpretations. (GS 374)

The world has "become infinite". Was it not infinite before? Of course it was; it was just that man before saw it from "out of his corner" and failed to recognise or admit or — why not? — cry for other corners.

So how does the world look from Nietzsche's corner? In another passage from the *Gay Science* called "Let us beware!" he warns us:

Let us beware of thinking the world is a living being. Whither should it spread itself? What should it nourish itself with? How could it grow and multiply?...

Let us likewise beware of believing the universe is a machine; it is certainly not constructed so as to perform some operation, we do it far too great an honour with the word 'machine'...

Let us beware of attributing to it heartlessness and unreason or their opposites: it is neither perfect nor beautiful nor noble, and has no desire to become any one of these; it is by no means striving to imitate mankind! It is quite impervious to all our aesthetic and moral judgements! It has likewise no impulse to self-preservation or impulses of any kind; neither does it know any laws. Let us beware of saying there are laws in nature. There are only necessities: there is no one to command, no one to obey, no one to transgress. When you realise that there are no goals or objectives, then you realise, too, that there is no chance: for only in a world of objectives does the word 'chance' have any meaning. Let us beware of saying that death is the opposite of life. The living being is only a species of the dead, and a very rare species. (GS 109)

Man wants to ascribe to the world what is running around through his own head. He wants it "humanised"; he wants it like himself; he wants to understand it the same way he understands himself. Let us beware of thinking we are talking about "the world", when we are really talking about ourselves.

Life no argument. — *We have arranged for ourselves a world in which we are able to live — with the postulation of bodies, lines, surfaces, causes and effects, motion and rest, form and content: without these articles of faith nobody could now endure to live! But that does not yet mean they are something proved and demonstrated. Life is no argument; among the conditions of life could be error. (GS 121)*

The fact that man is and has been around for a while does in no way mean that he holds the keys to what the world really is. Fish, goats, geese, and bacteria have probably shown equal or greater longevity and surely no one is going to venture that they "know" what "is". Nietzsche wants to put man in his place — wherever or whatever that may be. He wants us to stop deluding ourselves; if we don't or can't know what the world really is, let's face the music and at least dance in the dark with a well-lit conscience.

7

NIETZSCHE'S BEST GUESS: THE WILL TO POWER

Nietzsche does talk about the world being, at bottom, some kind of pushing and pulling of forces or "wills to power".

...Life itself is essentially appropriation, injury, overpowering of the strange and weaker, suppression, severity, imposition of one's own forms, incorporation and, at the least and mildest, exploitation... 'Exploitation' does not pertain to a corrupt or imperfect or primitive society: it pertains to the essence of the living thing as a fundamental organic function, it is a consequence of the intrinsic will to power which is precisely the will of life. (BGE 259)

But this will of life is not a will to preserve oneself as such:

To want to preserve oneself is the expression of a state of distress, a limitation of the actual basic drive of life, which aims at extension of power and in obedience to this will often enough calls self-preservation into question and sacrifices it. ...in nature the rule is not the state of distress, it is superfluity, prodigality, even to the point of absurdity. The struggle for existence is only an exception, a temporary restriction of the will of life; the struggle, great and small, everywhere turns on ascendancy, on growth and extension, in accordance with the will to power, which is precisely the will of life. (GS 349)

Growth, extension, prodigality, ascendancy, superfluity: these are the essence of the willing to power that Nietzsche sees at the bottom of life. What is is not, as a rule, struggling to be and stay what it is, but pushing to be more, to be other, to expand.

What is good? — All that heightens the feeling of power, the will to power, power itself in man. What is bad? — All that proceeds from weakness. What is happiness? — The feeling that power increases — that a resistance is overcome. (AC 2)

As with the problem of the "thinker" and the "thinking" (there is no "I" that "thinks"), we can naturally ask what is it that is "willing" to power? It seems that Nietzsche's best guess is much like that of the physicist in Geneva: There are no things, only forces; and what do forces do? They force, push, try to gain space, expand.

The world seen from within, the world described and defined according to its 'intelligible character' — it would be 'will to power' and nothing else. (BGE 36)

Hence we see Nietzsche's best guess as to the metaphysical guts of the world.

8

ONE THING IS CERTAIN: ANY NOTION OF "ANOTHER WORLD" OR A "HIGHER WORLD" OR "TRUER WORLD" OR "UNKNOWN WORLD" IS ANATHEMA TO NIETZSCHE

That this world cannot be known does not give licence to believing we can know another, other, higher, truer world. Here Nietzsche will bite the tongues off the world's prophets, seers, and revelators who long for another "real" realm of being. If we cannot know this life, how can we expect to know the "unknown".

But Heraclitus will always be right in this, that being is an empty fiction. The 'apparent' world (this world) is the only one: the 'real' world has only been lyingly added on..." (T, 'Reason in Philosophy', 2)

To repeat: "The 'real world', however one has hitherto conceived it — it has always been the apparent world once again." (WP 566)

Three types of men are responsible for bringing "another world" to this world:

The places of origin of the notion of 'another world': the philosopher, who invents a world of reason, where reason and logical functions are adequate: this is the origin of the 'true' world; the religious man, who invents a 'divine world': this is the origin of the 'denaturalized, anti-natural' world; the moral man, who invents a 'free world': this is the origin of the 'good, perfect, just holy' world. (WP 586)

Grasping what is being said here — like most things Nietzsche says — requires dropping to one's knees, not to pray, but to sniff the earth closer and with a finer nose than one has ever smelled with before, to imagine — to feel — that the world below, above, and horizontally is without any of the characteristics one has hitherto ascribed to it; i.e. it is neither true nor false, logical or illogical, real or unreal, free or unfree. None of these concepts apply to it; it is all natural, all unknowable, all a great necessity.

The concept 'the unknown world' insinuates that this world is 'known' to us (is tedious—); the concept 'another world' insinuates that the world could be otherwise — abolishes necessity and fate (useless to submit oneself — to adapt oneself —) the concept 'the true world' insinuates that this world is untruthful, deceptive, dishonest, inauthentic, inessential — and consequently also not a world adapted to our needs (inadvisable to adapt oneself to it; better to resist it). (WP 586)

There is no "unknown world" as there is no "known world"; there is no "other world" as nothing could be other than what it is; there is no "true world" as this world is never untrue in that only the human mind creates the true — false dichotomy, i.e. life itself cannot be untrue.

9

WHAT KIND OF PERSON WOULD DECLARE THAT THERE IS "ANOTHER", "BETTER", "HIGHER" WORLD THAT AWAITS US OR CAN BE ATTAINED?

The answer is so simple: the despisers of this world.

One does not say 'nothingness': one says 'the Beyond'; or 'God'; or 'true life'; or Nirvana, redemption, blessedness... This innocent rhetoric from the domain of religio-moral idiosyncrasy at once appears much less innocent when one grasps which tendency is here draping the mantle of sublime words about itself: the tendency hostile to life. (A 7)

The character of Dionysus in Nietzsche's philosophy can most clearly reveal — because Dionysus is the opposite — the type that is the metaphysician or religious man. At the end of his writing in *Ecce Homo* he says, "Have I been understood? — Dionysus against the Crucified..." The Crucified should not be understood to be Christ as such, but the religious man (including metaphysicians and all moralisers).

The religious man wants another world; Dionysus wants this world and this world only. Why? Because there is only this world. The religious man looks at this world and promises relief from suffering; Dionysus wants suffering because suffering is part of this world. The religious man says the world "ought" to be other than what it is; Dionysus says the world can't be other than what it is. Result: the religious man despises this world and longs for another; Dionysus loves this world and longs for nothing else. The religious man prays for something better, higher, truer, more moral, more beautiful; Dionysus sings and dances in the orgy of what is.

— What sets us apart is not that we recognize no God, either in history or in nature or behind nature – but that we find that which has been reverenced as God not 'godlike' but pitiable, absurd, harmful, not merely an error but a crime against life… (AC 49)

The last thing I would promise would be to 'improve' mankind. I erect no new idols; let the old idols learn what is means to have legs of clay. To overthrow idols (my word for 'ideals') — that rather is my business. Reality has been deprived of its value, its meaning, its veracity to the same degree as an ideal world has been fabricated... The 'real world' and the 'apparent world' — in plain terms: the fabricated world and reality... (EH 2) (Forward)

Affirmation of life even in its strangest and sternest problems; the will to life rejoicing in its own inexhaustibility through the sacrifice of its highest types — that is what I call Dionysian... (T, What I owe the Ancients, 5)

A spirit thus emancipated stands in the midst of the universe with a joyful and trusting fatalism, in the faith that only what is separate and individual may be rejected, that in the totality everything is redeemed and affirmed — he no longer denies. ... But such a faith is the highest of all possible faiths: I have baptized it with the name Dionysus." (I, Expeditions of an Untimely Man, 49)

The religious man has "faith" that this world will be redeemed, cleansed, gotten out of. His faith is in what isn't at the expense of what is. Dionysus, his opposite, has faith in his affirmation of what is, a yes to all that is because it could be nothing other than what it is. The religious man wants something else. Dionysus wants this; THIS and nothing else.

God degenerated to the contradiction of life, instead of being its transfiguration and eternal Yes! In God a declaration of hostility towards life, nature, the will to life! God the formula for every calumny of 'this world', for every lie about 'the next world'! In God nothingness deified, the will to nothingness sanctified! (A 18)

10

A FIRST LOOK AT MORALITY: WHAT IS IT? WHY THERE ARE NO MORAL PHENOMENA

Nietzsche's thoughts on morality derive directly from all the aforesaid, i.e. in a world of necessity, in a world in which "free" does not exist, morality makes no sense. This is not difficult to understand if we think that for us (most of us) we do not impute morality to the animal world or to what is commonly referred to as "nature". We do not say a lion is "immoral" for devouring an antelope. We do not attribute moral principles to a thunderbolt that ravishes a house or a human. Morality — good and evil — has no place in a world where "instincts" and "natural causes" reign. Well, for Nietzsche, man is part of that "natural" "instinctual" world. He is no more or less moral than the lion or the thunderbolt.

We do not accuse nature of immorality when it sends us a thunderstorm and makes us wet: why do we call the harmful man immoral? Because in the latter case we assume a voluntarily commanding free-will, in the former necessity. But this distinction is an error. (HA 102)

Nietzsche's world is not a kingdom of doers that do, of things that are and are acted upon. All is becoming, all is in flux, the wind does not blow, there is only blowing. A lion or a man is not an "it" with a soul that acts and chooses its actions any more than a cloud is a thing unchanging with a centre or soul that makes it do what it does. Human thinking has been laden with error that has led to the "moral" and "immoral" man, the "moral" and "immoral" civilisation. But, as Nietzsche says:

There are no moral phenomena at all, only a moral interpretation of phenomena... (BGE 108)

There are no moral phenomena because in Nietzsche's universe — where everything is nature — morality makes no sense. Historical man — in opposition to Nietzsche — defined human existence such that good and evil refer to something real. If man is free, he can choose between right and wrong. If God has established laws, then to live by them is moral and the contrary immoral. But Nietzsche's world lacks both free will and

God, hence to speak of moral or immoral is nonsense. To judge also is to not think...

...the philosopher thus has to say, as Christ did, 'judge not!' and the ultimate distinction between philosophical heads and the others would be that the former desire to be just, the others to be a judge. (AOM 33)

Here "to be just" is to see the world for what it is, i.e. infinite, unfathomable, becoming; "to be a judge" is to simplify, to be shallow, to accept the mind of the herd.

Herd instinct. — Where we encounter a morality we find a valuation and order of rank of human drives and actions. These valuations and orders of rank are always the expression of the needs of a community and herd: that which is its first requirement — and second and third — is also the supreme standard for the value of every individual. With morality the individual is led into being a function of the herd and to ascribing value to himself only as a function. As the conditions for the preservation of one community have been very different from those of another community, there have been very different

moralities; and considering the fundamental transformations of herds and communities, states and societies still to come, one can prophesy that there will be more very divergent moralities in the future. Morality is the herd instinct in the individual.
(GS 116)

To subject oneself to the morality of a herd and to believe that the herd and oneself are in the "good" is a human, all too human, thing to do. But a moment's reflection shows that to do so is highly "normal", but in no way "moral".

To become moral is not in itself moral. — Subjection to morality can be slavish or vain or self-interested or resigned or gloomily enthusiastic or an act of despair, like subjection to a prince: in itself it is nothing moral.
(Daybreak 97)

To resume:

1. Morality makes no sense in a world where all is necessity, i.e. everything is what it is and could be nothing other. Even to say this is misleading

because the "everything" is not really "thingness", but is a totality in flux, always becoming.

2. In such a world there is no free will. Morality depends on a belief in actors acting freely. Nietzsche doesn't believe this. Where, he asks, is the "I" that chooses or the "ego" that wills freely? Where is the "wind" that "blows".

3. The world is full of different moralities and there will be many more. To follow one is not to be moral, but to be traditional, i.e. to be part of a culture, society, tradition. Naturally the society — to preserve itself — says that its moral code is the true one, the real one, the absolute one, the right one. But they all say this.

Philosophers one and all have, with a strait-laced seriousness that provokes laughter, demanded something much higher, more pretentious, more solemn of themselves as soon as they have concerned themselves with morality as a science: they wanted to furnish the rational ground of morality — and every philosopher hitherto has believed he has furnished this rational ground; morality itself, however, was taken as 'given'. ...It was precisely because moral philosophers knew the facts of morality only somewhat vaguely in an arbitrary extract or as a chance abridgement, as morality of their environment, their class, their church, the spirit of their times, their climate, and zone of the earth, for instance — it was precisely because they were ill informed and not even very inquisitive about other peoples, ages, and former times, that they did not so much as catch sight of the real problems of morality — for these come into view only if we compare many moralities. Strange though it may sound, in all 'science of morals' hitherto the problem of morality itself has been lacking: the suspicion was lacking that there was anything problematic here. (BGE 186)

Philosophers always took for granted that morality itself made sense; their problem was simply *which* morality. Nietzsche says no morality is defensible because morality itself is the problem. Nature — everything — is beyond good and evil, or maybe before good and evil. That mankind (this curious corner of nature) has persisted in creating moralities is simply part of what this part of nature does. As Nietzsche says a bit later in *Beyond Good and Evil*:

Thou shalt obey someone and for a long time: otherwise thou shalt perish and lose all respect for thyself' — this seems to be nature's imperative, which is, to be sure, neither 'categorical' as old Kant demanded it should be (hence the 'otherwise' —), nor addressed to the individual (what do individuals matter to nature), but to peoples, races, ages, classes, and above all the entire animal 'man', to mankind. (BGE 188)

AN ASIDE FOR THE EARS OF PRESENT-DAY POLITICIANS

Inasmuch as ever since there have been human beings there have also been human herds (family groups, communities, tribes, nations, states, churches), and always very many who obey compared with the very small number of those who command — considering, that is to say, that hitherto nothing has been practiced and cultivated among men better or longer than obedience, it is fair to suppose that as a rule a need for it is by now innate as a kind of formal conscience which commands: 'thou shalt unconditionally do this, unconditionally not do that', in short 'thou shalt'. This need seeks to be satisfied and to fill out its form with a content; in doing so it grasps about wildly, according to the degree of its strength, impatience and tension, with little discrimination, as a crude appetite, and accepts what any commander — parent, teacher, law class prejudice, public opinion — shouts in its ears. The strange narrowness of human evolution, its hesitations, its delays, its frequent retrogressions and rotations, are due to the fact that the herd instinct of obedience has been inherited best and at the expense of the art of commanding. If we think of this instinct taken to its ultimate extravagance there would be no commanders or independent men at all; or, if they existed, they would suffer from a bad conscience and in order to be able to command would have to practice a deceit upon themselves: the deceit, that is, that they too were only obeying. This state of things actually exists in Europe today: I call it the moral hypocrisy of the commanders. They know no way of defending themselves against their bad conscience other than to pose as executors of more ancient or higher commands (commands of ancestors, of the constitution, of justice, of the law or even of God), or even to borrow herd maxims from the herd's way of thinking and appear as 'the first servant of the people' for example, or as 'instruments of the common good'. (BGE 199)

Having lived in Europe for twenty-two years and watched American politics from afar, but with eyes open, I can't help, but laugh — and cry — at how true Nietzsche's words are for the United States today. What leader commands? All I hear are voices grounded in God, opinion polls, the "Moral Majority", the Constitution (as if leaders in 1776 were sacred), the Bible, etc. etc. No leader commands that I know of. They only follow. Might this explain a little of

America's drop in prestige? In any case, passages like the one above not only help my digestion; they help paddle through the sea of contemporary political jabber.

11

MORALITY AND THE PSYCHOLOGY OF FREE WILL

For Nietzsche the notion of free will has been used by rulers, theologians in particular, to make man accountable to them and the tradition they want to maintain. One does not judge and punish nature, but the "free" man can be held accountable.

The error of free will. — We no longer have any sympathy today with the concept of 'free will': we know only too well what it is — the most infamous of all the arts of the theologian for making mankind 'accountable' in his sense of the word, that is to say for making mankind dependent on him... I give here only the psychology of making men accountable. — Everywhere accountability is sought, it is usually the instinct for punishing and judging which seeks it. One has deprived becoming of its innocence if being in this or that state is traced back to will, to intentions, to accountable acts: the doctrine of will has been invented essentially for the purpose of punishment, that is of finding guilty. The whole of the old-style psychology, the psychology of will, has as its precondition the desire of its authors, the priests at the head of the ancient communities, to create for themselves a right to ordain punishments — or their desire to create for God a right to do so... Men were thought of as 'free' so that they could become guilty: consequently, every action had to be thought of as willed, the origin of every action as lying in the consciousness (— whereby the most fundamental falsification in psychologicis *was made into the very principle of psychology)... Today, when we have started to move in the reverse direction, when we immoralists especially are trying with all our might to remove the concept of guilt and the concept of punishment from the world and to purge psychology, history, nature, the social institutions and sanctions of them, there is in our eyes no more radical opposition than that of the theologians, who continue to infect the innocence of becoming with 'punishment' and 'guilt' by means of the concept of the 'moral world order'. Christianity is a hangman's metaphysics... (TI, The Four Great Errors, 7)*

Before we look more closely at Nietzsche's view of Christianity, let us see the passage that follows in *Twilight of the Idols*. Here is an example of what

Nietzsche says in *The Anti-Christ*, i.e. *"I say in ten sentences what everyone else says in a book — what everyone else does not say in a book."*

What alone can our teaching be? — That no one gives a being his qualities: not God, not society, not his parents or ancestors, not he himself (— the nonsensical idea here last rejected was propounded, as 'intelligible freedom', by Kant, or perhaps also by Plato before him). No one is accountable for existing at all, or for being constituted as he is, or for living in the circumstances and surroundings in which he lives. The fatality of his nature cannot be disentangled from the fatality of all that which has been and will be. He is not the result of a special design, a will, a purpose; he is not the subject of an attempt to attain to an 'ideal of man' or an 'ideal of happiness' or an 'ideal of morality' — it is absurd to want to hand over his nature to some purpose or other. We invented the concept 'purpose': in reality purpose is lacking... One is necessary, one is a piece of fate, one belongs to the whole, one is in the whole — there exists nothing which could judge, measure, compare, condemn our being, for that would be to judge, measure, compare, condemn the whole... But nothing exists apart from the whole! That no one is any longer made accountable, that the kind of being

manifested cannot be traced back to a causa prima *(first cause), that the world is a unity neither as sensorium nor as 'spirit', this alone is the great liberation — thus alone is the innocence of becoming restored... The concept 'God' has hitherto been the greatest objection to existence... We deny God; in denying God, we deny accountability: only by doing that do we redeem the world. (TI, The Four Great Errors, 8)*

12

CHRISTIANITY IS NOT CHRIST

As we look torward Nietzsche's feelings about Christianity — and they are many and deep (his father was a pastor) — we must first be very clear that Nietzsche's attacks are not aimed at Christ, but at Christianity. He sees two distinct phenomena. In fact we shall come to understand that Nietzsche believes that Jesus Christ had many ideas very similar to his own. The man who wrote *The Anti-Christ* was probably trying to get our attention. I think we'll see that he really wrote "The Anti-Christian" or "Anti-Christianity". For him, what people did with Christ is as much an abomination as what, for me, the Nazis did with Nietzsche.

WHAT IS CHRISTIANITY FOR NIETZSCHE?

What Nietzsche berates in religion in general and Christianity in particular is that it hates what is. This world is not loved, embraced, "worshipped"; this world is held to be "impure", "imperfect", "sinful", something to be got over, something not good, something partial, a place to be looked past, an abortion of the real kingdom of God. Christianity wants this life to be sacrificed for "another life", this life needed to be "redeemed" by Christ, this life at the expense of a promised heaven. Such a teaching or belief is, for Nietzsche, anathema. It is man's greatest stupidity. First man took himself out of nature, then he took himself out of the world and aimed at another "higher" one.

In Christianity man's instincts, his "natural" propulsions, are bad. They are to be overcome, to be cleansed, purified. But for Nietzsche, what is to be overcome is just this kind of thinking, this kind of seeing man other than imperfectly. Life — man included — is what it is and can be nothing other. To see it otherwise is the greatest sin. Christianity promises the unreal at the expense of the real. Christianity despises what is (natural impulses, the body, man, life) and loves what isn't (heaven, the pure soul, the beyond). This is why Nietzsche calls religion in general — and Christianity in particular — decadent.

That the strong races of northern Europe have not repudiated the Christian God certainly reflects no credit on their talent for religion — not to speak of their taste. They ought to have felt compelled to have done with such a sickly and decrepit product of decadence. But there lies a curse on them for not having had done with it: they have taken up sickness, old age, contradiction into all their instincts — since then they have failed to create a God! Almost two millennia and not a single new God! (AC 19)

In Christianity neither morality, nor religion come into contact with reality at any point. Nothing, but imaginary causes ('God', 'soul', 'ego', 'spirit', 'free will' — or 'unfree will'): nothing but imaginary effects ('sin', 'redemption', 'grace', 'punishment', 'forgiveness of sins'). A traffic between imaginary beings ('God', 'spirit', 'souls'); ...an imaginary teleology ('the kingdom of God', 'the Last Judgement', 'eternal life') ... Once the concept 'nature' has been devised antithetical to 'God', 'natural' had to be the word for 'reprehensible' — this entire fictional world has its roots in hatred of the natural (— actuality! —), it is the expression of a profound discontent with the actual... But that explains everything. Who alone has reason to lie himself out of actuality? He who suffers from it. But to suffer from actuality means to be an abortive actuality... The preponderance of feelings of displeasure over feelings of pleasure is the cause of a fictitious morality and religion: such a preponderance, however, provides the formula for decadence... (AC 15)

The Christian conception of God — God of the sick, God as spider, God as spirit — is one of the most corrupt conceptions of God arrived at on earth: perhaps it even represents the low-water mark in the descending development of the God type... (AC 18)

If one shifts the centre of gravity of life out of life into the 'Beyond' — into nothingness — one has deprived life as such of its centre of gravity. The great lie of personal immortality destroys all rationality, all naturalness of instinct — all that is salutary, all that is life-furthering, all that holds a guarantee of the future in the instincts henceforth excites mistrust. So to live that there is no longer any meaning to living: that now becomes the 'meaning' of life...
(AC 43)

Christianity is so close to us, we are so imbued with it, that such passages must be read over and over again until one finally has a "feeling" for what Nietzsche is saying. All the foundations and promises and precepts of the Church have nothing to do with life, with the world, with what is. "God", "soul", "spirit", "redemption", "Last Judgment", "sin", "free will to choose good from evil", "grace of God", "punishment of God", "eternal life" etc... none of these has ever been proven by anybody to be real. None of them. For Nietzsche they have created a civilisation and culture that has decayed the instincts, has given man a false, guilty, sick image of himself and the world about him. If, in fact, man is not free as Nietzsche will have it, if, in fact, man is no different than the rest of nature as Nietzsche will have it, if, in fact, man is an unfathomable part and indistinguishable part of all being as Nietzsche will have it, if, in fact, there is no "beyond" "true" "heavenly" being as Nietzsche will have it, then... what then? Then we can see Christianity for what it is and has been: the human creation (we must say "a natural creation") which Nietzsche calls *"the one immortal blemish of mankind":*

...the extremest thinkable form of corruption, it has had the will to the ultimate corruption conceivably possible. The Christian Church has left nothing untouched by its depravity, it has made every value a disvalue, every truth a lie, of every kind of integrity a vileness of soul.... Parasitism as the sole practice of the Church; with its ideal of green-sickness, of 'holiness' draining away all blood, all love, all hope for life; the Beyond as the will to deny reality of every kind; the Cross as the badge of recognition for the most subterranean conspiracy there has ever been — a conspiracy against health, beauty, well-

constitutedness, bravery, intellect, benevolence of soul, against life itself... (AC 62)

This is philosophising with a hammer. Maybe it's necessary to get the message through. Big Church, big hammer.

Let us put Christianity in parentheses for a moment and imagine a Santa Claus Church. Santa's Church teaches the following:

1) Santa will give great presents to all the good boys and girls — after they die, that is.
2) Santa will give little or nothing to all the bad boys and girls.
3) The reason for this life is to get Santa's goodies in the next life.
4) Good boys and girls are good because they want to be good, i.e. they choose to be good.
5) Bad boys and girls are bad because they want to be bad i.e. they choose to be bad.
6) Santa's Father has never been seen, but he, Santa, was sent to earth and killed because boys and girls are naturally bad.
7) Santa's mother was an earthly type, but the father wasn't.

This, Nietzsche says, is the kind of stuff that has dominated our civilisation for two thousand years. This is what the human head has held. This is the "holiness" that has drained the blood from the human herd.

JESUS (TO SAY IT AGAIN) IS NOT CHRISTIANITY

What did Christ deny? Everything that is today called Christian. (WP 158)

Christianity (Christ) is a way of life, not a system of beliefs. It tells us how to act, not what we ought to believe. (WP 212)

In the entire psychology of the 'Gospel' the concept guilt and punishment is lacking; likewise the concept reward. Sin, every kind of distancing relationship between God and man, is abolished — precisely this is the 'glad tidings'. Blessedness is not promised, it is not tied to any conditions: it is the only reality — the rest is signs for speaking of it...

The consequence of such a condition projects itself into a new practice, the true evangelic practice. It is not a 'belief' which distinguishes the Christian: the Christian acts, he is distinguished by a different mode of acting. Neither by words nor in his heart does he resist the man who does him evil. He makes no distinction between foreigner and native, between Jew and non-Jew (one's 'neighbour' is properly one's co-religionist, the Jew). He is not angry with anyone, does not distain anyone... — All fundamentally one law, all consequences of one instinct. —

The life of the redeemer was nothing else than this practice — his death too was nothing else... He no longer required any formulas, any rites for communicating with God — not even prayer... It is not 'penance', not 'prayer for forgiveness' which leads to God: evangelic practice alone leads to God, it is God! What was abolished with the Evangel was the Judaism of the concepts 'sin', 'forgiveness of sin', 'faith', 'redemption by faith' — the whole of the Jewish ecclesiastical teaching was denied in the 'glad tidings'. (AC 33)

His words to the thief on the cross contain the whole Evangel. 'That was verily a divine man, a child of God!' — says the thief. 'If thou feelest this' — answers the redeemer — 'thou art in Paradise, thou are a child of God.' Not to defend oneself, not to grow angry, not to make responsible... But not to resist even the evil man — to love him... (AC 35)

For Nietzsche, Jesus's death was also the death of Christianity. What followed had little or nothing to do with what his life had been.

— To resume, I shall now relate the real history of Christianity. —The word 'Christianity' is already a misunderstanding — in reality there has been only one Christian, and he died on the Cross. What was called 'Evangel' died on the Cross. What was called 'Evangel' from this moment onwards was already the opposite of what he had lived: 'bad tidings', a dysangel. (AC 39)

When Christ died the disciples had to come up with a "logic", a sense, a meaning for his death. Here Nietzsche sees the beginning of the end of Christianity.

Clearly the little community had failed to understand precisely the main thing, the exemplary element in his (Christ's) manner of dying, the freedom from, the superiority over every feeling of ressentiment: a sign of how little they understood of him at all! Jesus himself could have desired nothing by his death, but publicly to offer the sternest test, the proof of his teaching… But his disciples were far from forgiving his death — which would have been evangelic in the highest sense; not to speak of offering themselves up to a similar death in sweet and gentle peace of heart... Precisely the most unevangelic of feelings, revengefulness, again came uppermost. The affair could not possibly be at an end with his death: one required 'retribution', 'judgement' (and yet what can be more unevangelic than 'retribution', 'punishment', 'sitting in judgement'?) The popular expectation of a Messiah came once more into the foreground; an historic moment appeared in view: the 'kingdom of God' is coming to sit in judgement on its enemies... But with this everything is misunderstood... (AC 40)

— And now an absurd problem came up: 'How could God have permitted that?' For this question the deranged reason of the little community found a downright terrifyingly absurd answer: God gave his son for the forgiveness of sins, as a sacrifice. All at once it was all over with the Gospel! The guilt sacrifice, and that in its most repulsive, barbaric form, the sacrifice of the innocent man for the sins of the guilty! What atrocious paganism! — For Jesus had done away with the concept 'guilt' itself — he had denied any chasm between God and man, he lived this unity of God and man as his 'glad tidings' ...the whole and sole reality of the Evangel, is juggled away

— for the benefit of a state after death!... Paul, with that rabbinical insolence which characterizes him in every respect, rationalized this interpretation, this indecency of an interpretation, thus: 'If Christ is not resurrected from the dead our faith is vain'. — All at once the Evangel became that most contemptible of all unfulfillable promises, the impudent doctrine of personal immortality... Paul himself even taught it as a reward! (AC 41)

And if I dare say, "the rest is history". What followed was and is nothing but a series of lies, fabrications, errors, untruths, imaginary causes, imaginary effects, imaginary theologies, and decadence that has sapped man of his strength, "sucked his blood", and has left him far, far, far from whatever string of "truth" he might otherwise have been capable of grabbing onto.

The Gospel Jesus brought was free of guilt, punishment, and resentment. It was a love of the here and now, the within: *"If thou feelest this, thou art in Paradise."* Interestingly traces of this are in Nietzsche. His world leaves no place for guilt. Guilt makes no sense in a universe of necessity. And as we will see at the end, Nietzsche's final call was a *"Yes"* to all that has been, is, and will be. Jesus seems somewhat a bedfellow.

13

PITY: WHY NIETZSCHE THINKS IT'S A NEGATIVE FORCE

Before turning from his thoughts on Christianity, we must see how pity has nothing but negative consequences for Nietzsche. He sees pity as a source of perpetuation of weakness. He who feels pity loses strength and he who is pitied is defended in his state of decadence, i.e. in his loss of life force.

Pity stands in antithesis to the tonic emotions which enhance the energy of the feeling of life: it has a depressive effect. One loses force when one pities. The loss of force which life has already sustained though suffering is increased and multiplied even further by it. Suffering itself becomes contagious through pity: sometimes it can bring about a collective loss of life and life-energy which stands in an absurd relation to the quantum of its cause (- the case of the death of the Nazarene). This is the first aspect; but there is an even more important one. If one judges pity by the value of the reactions which it usually brings about, its morally dangerous character appears in a much clearer light. Pity on the whole thwarts the law of evolution, which is the law of selection. It preserves what is ripe for destruction; it defends life's disinherited and condemned; though the abundance of the ill-constituted of all kinds which it retains in life it gives life itself a gloomy and questionable aspect. ...To say again, this depressive and contagious instinct thwarts those instincts bent on preserving and enhancing the value of life: both as a multiplier of misery and a conservator of everything miserable it is one of the chief instruments for the advancement of decadence — pity persuades to nothingness! ...Nothing in our unhealthy morality is more unhealthy than Christian pity. (AC 7)

Pity, like Christianity, is a way of saying "no" to what is. Nietzsche does not want gloom, he does not want to wallow in misery, he does not want to perpetuate weakness; he wants to look being in the face and say "yes" — not "yes" to part of it, but "yes" to the whole, unfathomable, unknowable, necessity.

WHICH LEADS US TOWARDS HIS NOTION OF THE SUPERMAN ...

INTERMEZZO

A FEW MAXIMS AND ARROWS FROM
TWILIGHT OF THE IDOLS

Even the bravest of us rarely has the courage for what he really knows...

To live alone one must be an animal or a god — says Aristotle. There is yet a third case: one must be both — a philosopher.

'All truth is simple.' — Is that not a compound lie?

Which is it? Is man only God's mistake or God only man's mistake?

From the military school of life. — What does not kill me makes me stronger.

Help thyself: then everyone will help thee too. Principle of Christian charity.

Let us not be cowardly in the face of our actions! Let us not afterwards leave them in the lurch! —
Remorse of conscience is indecent.

In order to look for beginnings one becomes a crab. The historian looks backwards; at last he also believes backwards.

I mistrust all systematizers and avoid them. The will to a system is a lack of integrity.

If a woman possesses manly virtues one should run away from her; and if she does not possess them she runs away herself.

You run on ahead? Do you do so as a herdsman? Or as an exception? A third possibility would be as a deserter... First question of conscience.

Are you genuine? Or only an actor? A representative? Or that itself which is represented? — Finally you are no more than an imitation of an actor... Second question of conscience.

The disappointed man speaks. — I sought great human beings, I never found anything but the apes of their ideal.

Are you one who looks on? Or who sets to work? — or who looks away, turns aside... Third question of conscience.

Do you went to accompany? Or go on ahead? Or go off alone? ...One must know what one wants and that one wants. — Fourth question of conscience.

For me they were steps, I have climbed up upon them — therefore I had to pass over them. But they thought I wanted to settle down on them...

Formula of my happiness: a Yes, a No, a straight line, a goal...

14

TOWARD THE "SUPERMAN" OR "OVERMAN" OR WHATEVER YOU WANT TO CALL HIM

Nietzsche is telling us that man has been duped: he has believed in untruth; he has followed moralities that were founded in nothing other than tradition and expedience; he has worshipped decadent gods; he has attributed to himself qualities that are unreal (ego, free will, knower); he has taken himself out of "nature" and has created universe of Santa Clauses and Easter Bunnies and Judges and Moralists; he has devalued himself and this world; he has set up absurd dichotomies (apparent-real, life-death, good-evil, man-nature, instinct-soul, inner-outer, mind-body, matter-spirit, that have given him a false sense of who he is and what the world is; he has been a follower of phony prophets, phony philosophers and phony gods, and the prophets and philosophers themselves have been followers; he has seen himself as other than perfect, i.e. he has thought he ought to be other than what he is and that he and his world were to be gotten over or gotten past and in some way "redeemed" and rid of; he has been a nay-sayer and not a yes-sayer; he has seen being where there is only becoming, i.e. he has wanted the world to be "something" when in fact all is always in flux; he has wanted that "something" to be in his image — he has tried to give meaning and purpose to the world like he gives meaning and purpose to his own life, but here again he fools himself because the world Nietzsche sees has no purpose or meaning, this having no purpose and meaning is not to be seen as nihilism, but on the contrary is a liberating thing because were there purpose and meaning to the world man would be a slave to this purpose and meaning, but since there isn't such a thing man is "free" in the most profound sense.

What man or men have really been thus free? Nietzsche asks. He sees very few. He sometimes talks of Goethe or Napoleon. His superman or overman or higher man is just this kind of man. He is one who is not deluded, but who looks the world in the eyes and says, "Ah, so this is what you are you player of 'hide and seek', this is what you are and you could be nothing other, and I will love you."

Nietzsche's passage in *The Gay Science* called "The Madman" gives a sign as to what higher man is coming. The passage has been quoted to death but brings life here:

The madman. — *Have you not heard of that madman who lit a lantern in the bright morning hours, ran to the marketplace and cried incessantly: 'I am looking for God! I am looking for God!' — As many of those who did not believe in God were standing together there he excited considerable laughter. Have you lost him then? Said one. Did he lose his way like a child? Said another. Or is he hiding? Is he afraid of us? Has he gone on a voyage? Or emigrated? — thus they shouted and laughed. The madman sprang into their midst and pierced them with his glances. 'Where has God gone?' he cried. 'I shall tell you. We have killed him — you and I. We are all his murderers. But how have we done this? How were we able to drink up the sea? Who gave us the sponge to wipe away the entire horizon? What did we do when we unchained this earth from its sun? Whither is it moving now? Whither are we moving now? Away from all suns? Are we not perpetually falling? Backward, sideward, forward, in all directions? Is there any up or down left? Are we not straying as if through an infinite nothing? Do we not feel the breath of empty space? Has it not become colder? Is more and more night not coming on all the time? Must not lanterns be lit in the morning? Do we not hear anything yet of the noise of the gravediggers who are burying God? Do we not smell anything yet of God's decomposition?*

— gods, too, decompose. God is dead. God remains dead. And we have killed him. How shall we, the murderers of all murderers, console ourselves? That which was holiest and mightiest of all that the world has yet possessed has bled to death under our knives — who will wipe this blood off us? With what water could we purify ourselves? What festivals of atonement, what sacred games shall we need to invent? Is not the greatness of this deed too great for us? Must we not ourselves become gods simply to seem worthy of it? There has never been a greater deed — and whosoever shall be born after us, for the sake of this deed he shall be part of a higher history than all history hitherto.' Here the madman fell silent and again regarded his listeners; and they, too, were silent and stared at him in astonishment. At last he threw his lantern to the ground and it broke and went out. 'I come too early,' he said then; 'my time has not yet come. This tremendous event is still on its way, still travelling – it has not yet reached the ears of men. Lightning and thunder require time, deeds require time after they have been done before they can be seen and heard. This deed is still more distant from them than the most distant stars — and yet they have done it themselves.' — It has been related further that on the same day the madman entered diverse churches and there sang a requiem aeternam deo. Led out and quieted, he is said to have retorted each

time: *'What are these churches now if they are not tombs and sepulchers of God?' (GS 125)*

"This tremendous event is still on its way, still travelling – it has not yet reached the ears of men."

"Must we not ourselves become gods simply to seem worthy of it?"

Nietzsche's vision is still on its way; the higher type of man takes time; it takes time to become a god.

Do you call yourself free? I want to hear your idea, and not that you have escaped from a yoke. Are you such a man as ought to escape a yoke? There are many who threw off their final worth when they threw off their bondage.

Free from what? Zarathustra does not care about that! But your eye should clearly tell me: free for what?

Can you furnish yourself with your own good and evil and hang up your own will above yourself as a law? Can you be judge of yourself and avenger of your law?

It is terrible to be alone with the judge and avenger of one's own law. It is to be like a star thrown forth into empty space and into the icy breath of solitude. (Z I, Of the Way of the Creator)

It is easy to see that a higher man is someone who will go right where men in the past have gone wrong. He will not follow; he will not be judged by other men's laws. He will be part of a higher history than all history hitherto. He will not be free from, but will be free for... for one: free for laughter, for a dancing spirit that laughs.

You higher men, the worst about you is: none of you has learned to dance as a man ought to dance — to dance beyond yourselves! What does it matter that you are failures!

How much is still possible! So learn to laugh beyond yourselves! Lift up your hearts, you fine dancers, high! higher! and do not forget to laugh well. This laughter's crown, this rose-wreath crown: to you, my brothers, do I throw this crown! I have canonized laughter: you higher men, learn — to laugh! (Z IV, Of Higher Man 19-20)

...for another: *free for play, free for life's little pleasures now that the heaviness of God, sin, truth, virtue, and the Beyond have been buried in soft graves.* I quote in full passage 10 from the chapter "Why I Am So Clever" in Nietzsche's autobiography *Ecce Homo*.

I shall be asked why I have really narrated all these little things which according to the traditional judgment are matters of indifference: it will be said that in doing so I harm myself all the more if I am destined to fulfill great tasks. Answer: these little things — nutriment, place, climate, recreation, the whole casuistry of selfishness — are beyond all conception of greater importance than anything that has been considered of importance hitherto. It is precisely here that one has to begin to learn anew. Those things which mankind has hitherto pondered seriously are not even realities, merely imaginings, more strictly speaking lies from the bad instincts of sick, in the profoundest sense injurious natures – all the concepts 'God', 'soul', 'virtue', 'sin', 'the Beyond', 'truth', 'eternal life'... But the greatness of human nature, its 'divinity', has been sought in them ... All questions of politics, the ordering of society, education have been falsified down to their foundations because the most injurious men have been taken for great men — because contempt has been taught for the 'little' things, which is to say for the fundamental affairs of life ... Now, when I compare myself with the men who have hitherto been honored as pre-eminent men the distinction is palpable. I do not count these supposed 'pre-eminent men' as belonging to mankind at all – to me they are the refuse of mankind, abortive offspring of sickness and revengeful instincts: they are nothing but pernicious, fundamentally incurable monsters, who take revenge on life ... I want to be the antithesis of this: it is my privilege to possess the highest subtlety for all the signs of healthy instincts. Every morbid trait is lacking in me; even in periods of severe illness. I did not become morbid; a trait of fanaticism will be sought in vain in my nature. At no moment of my life can I be shown to have adopted any kind of arrogant or pathetic posture. The pathos of attitudes does not belong to greatness; whoever needs attitudes does not belong to greatness; whoever needs attitudes at all is false... Beware of all picturesque men! — Life has been easy for me, easiest when it demanded of me the most difficult things. Anyone who saw me during the seventy days of this autumn when I was uninterruptedly creating nothing but things of the first rank which no man will be able to do again, or has done before, bearing a responsibility for all the coming millennia, will have noticed no trace of tension in me, but rather an overflowing freshness

and cheerfulness. I never ate with greater relish, I never slept better. — I know of no other way of dealing with great tasks than that of play: this is, as a sign of greatness, an essential precondition. The slightest constraint, the gloomy mien, any kind of harsh note in the throat are all objections to a man, how much more to his work!... One must have no nerves... to suffer from solitude is likewise an objection. I have always suffered only from the 'multitude' ... At an absurdly early age, at the age of seven, I already knew that no human word would ever reach me: has anyone ever seen me sad on that account? — Still today I treat everyone with the same geniality, I am even full of consideration for the basest people: in all this there is not a grain of arrogance, of secret contempt. He whom I despise divines that I despise him: through my mere existence I enrage everything that has bad blood in its veins... My formula for greatness in a human being is amor fati: *that one wants nothing to be other than it is, not in the future, not in the past, not in all eternity. Not merely to endure that which happens of necessity, still less to dissemble it — all idealism is untruthfulness in the face of necessity — but to love it...*
(EH, Why I Am So Clever, 10)

Nietzsche can write of himself that he created things which "no man will be able to do again" and no man "has done before" and at the same time say that in him "there is not a grain of arrogance". This is because he — the higher man — understands the "he" is not "his own doing", but is a part of the necessity that is all becoming. He is a moment in eternity that is not good or evil or true or untrue, but he is a revealer of the potential for, if not the fact of, a new kind of man who has a new feeling for life. *Amor fati*. A love of all as it is, has been and will be because nothing can be other than what it is. Nietzsche himself knows he is a part of destiny, that he too is necessity like the "basest people" for whom he is full of consideration. He shouts arrows and throws darts at Christians and moralisers and idealists, but he knows that they too are but a part of fate. He is the part that is ushering in something else, something less deluded, less duped.

I know my fate. One day there will be associated with my name the recollection of something frightful — of a crisis like no other before on earth, of the profoundest collision of conscience, of a decision evoked against everything that until them had been believed in, demanded, sanctified. I am not a man, I am dynamite. — And with all that there is nothing in me of a founder of a religion — religions are affairs of the rabble, I have need of washing my hands after contact with religious people... I do not want 'believers', I think I am too malicious to believe in myself, I never speak to masses... I have a terrible fear that I shall one day be pronounced holy: one will guess why I bring out this book beforehand; it is intended to prevent people from making mischief with me... I do not want to be a saint, rather even a buffoon... Perhaps I am a buffoon ... And nonetheless, or rather not nonetheless — for there has hitherto been nothing more mendacious than saints — the truth speaks out of me. — But my truth is dreadful: for hitherto the lie has been called truth. Revaluation of all values: this is my formula for an act of supreme coming-to-oneself on the part of mankind which in me has become flesh and genius. It is my fate to have to be the first decent human being, to know myself in opposition to the mendaciousness of millennia ... I was the first to discover the truth, in that I was the first to sense — smell — the lie as lie ... My genius is in my nostrils ... I contradict as has never been contradicted and am nonetheless the opposite of a negative spirit. I am a bringer of good tidings such as there has never been... With all that I am necessarily a man of fatality. For when truth steps into battle with the lie of millennia we shall have convulsions, an earthquake spasm, a transposition of valley and mountain such as has never been dreamed of...

I am by far the most terrible human being there has ever been; this does not mean I shall not be the most beneficent. I know joy in destruction to a degree corresponding to my strength for destruction — in both I obey my Dionysian nature, which does not know how to separate No-doing from Yes-saying. I am the first immoralist: I am there with the destroyer par excellence. (EH, Why I Am a Destiny, 1-2)

When Nietzsche says, *"Behold, I teach you the superman: he is this lightening, he is this madness",* he speaks of the lightening that strikes and sets fire to the truths and values of millennia and the madness that is the Dionysian vision that embraces all suffering, all joy, all becoming, and says yes, O yes. He says,

I want to wage no war against the ugly. I do not want to accuse, I do not want to accuse even the accusers. May looking away be my only form of negation! And, all in all: I want to be at all times hereafter only an affirmer!
(GS 276)

15

THE ETERNAL RETURN: TWO INTERPRETATIONS

Much has been said and made of Nietzsche's "theory" of the Eternal Return. Is it really a theory, something new? Or is it a simple extension of what has heretofore been said? It seems there are two distinct possibilities as to what Nietzsche meant by Eternal Return.

First it may be thought that a passage like the following is to be taken literally:

The heaviest burden. — What if a demon crept after you one day or night in your loneliest solitude and said to you: 'This life, as you live it now and have lived it, you will have to live it again and again, times without number; and there will be nothing new in it, but every pain and every joy and every thought and sigh and all the unspeakably small and great in your life must return to you, and everything in the same series and sequence — and in the same way this spider and this moonlight among the trees, and in the same way this moment and I myself. The eternal hourglass of existence will be turned again and again — and you with it, you dust of dust!' — Would you not throw yourself down and gnash your teeth and curse the demon who thus spoke? Or have you experienced a tremendous moment in which you would have answered him: 'You are a god and never did I hear anything more divine!' (GS 341)

Taken at its word, this passage would seem to mean that:

a) Nietzsche sees the stuff of the universe to be a fixed, finite amount.
b) Time, however, is infinite.
c) Given that all things are chained together in a great necessity, all that can happen in the chain will happen and when the cycle is complete, everything will start up and happen again ad infinitum.

This is a possible interpretation of the meaning of the eternal return. It is a literal interpretation, but a plausible one given the above passage, or the following:

"Now I die and decay," you would say, "and in an instant I shall be nothingness. Souls are as mortal as

bodies.

"But the complex of causes in which I am entangled will recur — it will create me again! I myself am part of these causes of the eternal recurrence.

"I shall return, with this sun, with this earth, with this eagle, with this serpent – not to a new life or a better life or a similar life:

"I shall return eternally to this identical and selfsame life, in the greatest things and in the smallest, to teach once more the eternal recurrence of all things, to speak once more the teaching of the great noontide of earth and man, to tell him of the superman once more.

"I spoke my teaching, I broke upon my teaching: thus my eternal fate will have it — as prophet do I perish." (Z III, The Convalescent)

Does Nietzsche want us to think of the Eternal Return as the words here paint it, or is he simply trying to get us to feel — perhaps more deeply than ever before — that all that is could be and will be nothing other than what it is for all eternity. And if this is so, the vision of the superman is to say "yes" to all of it, yes to the greatest and the smallest, yes to the greatest joy and the greatest suffering, yes to noon and yes to midnight, yes to yesterday, today and tomorrow, yes to eternity:

Did you ever say Yes to one joy? O my friends, then you said Yes to all woe as well. All things are chained and entwined together, all things are in love; if ever you wanted one moment twice, if ever you said: 'You please me, happiness, instant, moment!' then you wanted everything to return! You wanted everything anew, everything eternal, everything chained, entwined together, everything in love, oh that is how you loved the world, you everlasting men, loved it eternally and for all time: and you say even to woe: 'Go, but return!' For all joy wants — eternity!

...For all joy wants itself, therefore it also wants heart's agony! O happiness! O pain! O break heart! You higher men, learn this, learn that joy wants eternity, joy wants the eternity of all things, wants deep, deep, deep eternity!

Have you learned my song? Have you divined what it means? Very well! Come on! You higher men, now sing my roundelay!

Now sing yourselves the song whose name is "Once more", whose meaning is 'To all eternity!' — sing, you higher men, Zarathustra's roundelay!

O Man! Attend!
What does deep midnight's voice contend?
'I slept my sleep,
'And now awake at dreaming's end:
'The world is deep,

'Deeper than day can comprehend.
'Deep is its woe,
'Joy – deeper than heart's agony:
'Woe says: Fade! Go!
'But all joy wants eternity,
'Wants deep, deep, deep eternity!'

(Z IV, The Drunken Song 9-11)

In Nietzsche's vision — is there another word than "vision"? — to say "yes" to one single moment is to say "yes" to everything because that one single moment could not and would not have been if everything else had not been because "all things are chained and entwined together". This is the vision of eternity: To want one moment is to want it all, forever and ever. Does "Forever and ever" come back again? I don't know, but I'm not sure it matters in Nietzsche's vision. What matters might be the "saying yes", the "wanting", the drunkard singing Zarathustra's roundelay...

16

BREAKFAST APPROACHES ITS END

Before we clear the table of all the bowls, plates, coffee cups, and breadcrumbs, I want to be sure the stomachs are full enough, but not stuffed. Breakfast is a lightish meal. Too much makes us heavy, too little and legs are weak.

So what have we been fed?

Interestingly, Nietzsche has often been called a "nihilist". Nothing could be farther from the truth. Clarifying this cloudiness is a way to resume all that's been heretofore said.

Nietzsche did tear down many walls. He had to. He had to knock down the building in order to build his nest. He did not want a temple, nor worshippers, nor followers. He did not want a system because systems simplify and lie. Though the youngest professor at Basel University, he stopped teaching after a couple of years and wandered Europe writing his books and thinking his thoughts. He wanted the air and light of Engadine and Italy. He wanted his solitude to nurture his loneliest thoughts. It is said that he was a gentle, polite man wherever he went.

Nietzsche's vision was the opposite of the nihilist's. For him the "Christians", moralists, pessimists, naysayers, and despisers of this life were the true nihilists. They wanted and worshipped another world. Nietzsche wants this world. And he wants it all. He tore down the walls of religion, morality and metaphysics in order to become the great affirmer of this world.

It seems to me that many Nietzsche readers get lost in the noise when he was wielding the hammer and cracking the old statues. They fail to get past the ruins and into Nietzsche's nesting ground. He wrote much and about many things. I have tried to provide what I feel is the essential — enough to start the day. Lunch and dinner you must hunt yourself.

In any case, Nietzsche did not want "Nietzschians": he wanted no followers, no church, no congregation. He cannot tell you how to be. Every being — man included — is unique; in fact no being is even identical to itself; all is in flux. To even call Nietzsche "Nietzsche" probably misses the point. What comes out of his writing is a vision that I have tried to begin to convey. Perhaps as we clear the table, the world might look a bit different than it did when we started our breakfast. He wanted the blood and guts of existence — no veils, no myths, no false remedies, no lies, no promises. He ripped off the band-aids that previous thinkers, moralisers and meta-doctors had wrapped round the world. He wanted the raw meat:

I know my fate. One day there will be associated with my name the recollection of something frightful — of a crisis like no other before on earth, of the profoundest collision of conscience, of a decision evoked against everything that until then had been believed in, demanded, sanctified. I am not a man, I am dynamite. (EH, Why I Am a Destiny)

And after his bomb has ignited and the dust has settled, the echo of Zarathustra's roundelay returns to our ears:

O man! Attend!
What does deep midnight's voice contend?
I slept my sleep,
And now awake at dreaming's end:
The world is deep,
Deeper than day can comprehend.
Deep is its woe,
Joy – deeper than heart's agony:
Woe says: Fade! Go!
But all joy wants eternity,
Wants deep, deep, deep eternity!

_____

BOOKS BY JON FERGUSON

(Published by Huge Jam)

Adam's Cane
Foster's Depression
The Last Day Forever
Jesus & Mary
Mary & God
God & Naomi
The Flood
The Anthropologist
Three Forgotten Tales
Nietzsche for Breakfast
Burnt Roses
Don't Bullshit Me Daddy

www.hugejam.com
www.jonfergusonbooks.com

ABOUT THE AUTHOR

Jon Ferguson was born in October 1949 in Oakland, California, into a devout Christian family, much like his favorite philosopher, Friedrich Nietzsche. In fact, as a child, church services were held in the family living room. At age 17, his passion for sport was almost usurped by a keenness to save the world when he enrolled at the Mormon-owned Brigham Young University. Little by little, though, he realized that if Jesus couldn't do it, neither could he. His faith in divinity began to crumble. With an adieu to the US academic world where he'd been immersed in anthropology and philosophy – and with a desire to engage with the world at large – Ferguson hopped on a plane in 1973 and by chance ended up in Nyon, Switzerland where he was soon playing basketball in the top Swiss league, becoming a key player in what fans consider to have been the golden age.

Half a century later, still in Switzerland, he is now just as well known for his writing (eighteen books published in French) as for his coaching (thirty years' worth). He won more games than any coach in Swiss basketball history, but he likes to remind people that he lost more than everyone else as well... He has written over twenty novels and a book on Nietzsche, Nietzsche au Petit Déjeuner ("Nietzsche for Breakfast") and a book on the history of Swiss basketball, Of Hoops and Men. For twenty-five years he also wrote a bi-weekly column in the Lausanne newspaper called "Ainsi Parla Schmaltz". His novel Farley's Jewel (Cinco Puntos Press, 1998) won a Barnes & Noble "Discover Great New Writers of America" prize.

Find out more:
www.jonfergusonbooks.com

Find out more about Jon Ferguson
and his works at his author website:
www.jonfergusonbooks.com,
where you can also sign up for updates.

Please contribute an honest online review;
it's the easiest and most supportive thing a reader can do
for an author and/or a small independent press.
editor@hugejam.com

www.ingramcontent.com/pod-product-compliance
Lightning Source LLC
Chambersburg PA
CBHW012005090526
44590CB00026B/3889